The Poet's Corner

A place for your heart!

Vrinda Ramesh

BookLeaf Publishing
India | USA | UK

Made with ❤ on the BookLeaf Publishing Platform
www.bookleafpub.in
www.bookleafpub.com

Dedication

Dedicated to Saraswati Maa!

Thank you for endowing me with the knowledge to write this book!

Dedicated to my entire family and readers.

Preface

Poetry, to me, has always been a form of quiet rebellion —an intimate act of capturing the unsaid and immortalizing fleeting moments. Over the years, I have poured my heart into these verses, allowing them to be vessels of my deepest emotions and reflections. These poems are not just words on a page; they are my soul stretched out in ink, a mosaic of my lifetime's musings. Within these pages, you will find poetry that echoes the rhythm of nature's song, contemplates the fragility and beauty of life and death, delves into the epic tales of Hindu mythology, and revives the spirit of historic incidents that have shaped our beloved India. Each poem stands as a testament to the awe, sorrow, and wonder I have encountered on this journey.

This book is not merely a collection; it is an invitation—an invitation to pause, to feel, and to awaken the inner poet within you. My hope is that these poems will not just delight your senses, but will stir something profound within you—a spark, a memory, or perhaps a sense of connection to the universe that cradles us all.

Thank you for joining me on this poetic expedition. May these verses find a home in your heart, as they have in mine.

Acknowledgements

Writing this book has been a deeply personal and transformative experience, and it would not have been possible without the support and encouragement of several remarkable individuals.

First and foremost, I would like to thank my mom for their unwavering belief in me and this project. Your kindness and encouragement have been the foundation upon which this book stands.

To my dad, whose insights, guidance, and mentorship shaped my understanding and gave me the confidence to bring this vision to life—thank you for inspiring me to keep going even when the path seemed unclear.

A heartfelt thanks to my sister and my grandmothers for their constructive feedback, patience, and invaluable support throughout the writing process. Your words of encouragement and thoughtful critiques brought out the very best in this book.

Finally, to the readers, thank you for embracing these pages and for allowing me to share my thoughts and emotions with you. This book exists because of your openness and your love for the written word.

1. Music

The wind howls
The sea growls
But what is common?
They all make sounds

The birds chirp.
Their babies lurk
The leaves flutter
Though they are cluttered
All of them utter
To make these sounds

The people talk
The chairs, they rock
The haters, they mock
The dogs, they bark
All of them
They are sounds

Sounds, they join

to make a tune
Just like smoke
Gets formed by fumes

Music is vast
With an ancient past
Forever they last
They Evolve fast

Nature is the best musician
Natural sounds
Join together.
Make a sound.

2. The Race of Life

In the Race of life,
Remember past will make you last
Move on from things sacrificed
For you must catch up in this race fast.

Move on from things left
Move on from money theft
Forget if you in the past chose right or left
Learn from errors, old and other memories must be swept
People come and people go,
Accept this fact and you move on too,
Theres no harm in going solo,
People who mock, are jealous of you

To every lock,
There is a key
Hardwork is needed
For everything you see

These few things,
You must keep in mind
With a happy smile
You must pass through life

3. Eternal Truth

What if the world turned upright?
Would we be soaring in the sky like a kite?
Would people be selfless and be nice and kind?
Why do people stare at darkness when there is light?

Oh lord! I wish to be granted sight
He is all inside, why do we stare outside?
Why can't there be peace? Why do we always fight?
But when we face our darkest fears, its never 'fight' but
'flight'

What if we never got into a plight?
What if people always did what was right?
Would we rather be blinded by the day that is bright?
Or be engulfed in the darkness emitted during the night?

All these questions have the same answer.
That one eternal truth we must all conquer.
Understand what the actual purpose is of life,
This eternal truth will help you get through this strife.

4. Life

A blissful morning, a wave of breeze,
The warmth that fills within.
The expanse of blue, The shining sun,
The peach colour of our skin.

None of this ever bothers us,
Only take and give.
An egoistic point of view,
Covers the way to live.

It is as if this will stay forever,
When it's of no use when we die
Time is precious, Life is short,
Our aim is very high.

Do we ever realise?
The importance of our life.
Time is less but all we care,
Is creating unnecessary strife.

5. Success and Failure

Is life unfair? Is life a misery?
Going through obstacles is not everyone's cup of tea
Even the waves of the sea, crash on the rocks.
Let us find a key for this lock

Don't get angry if you lose or fall
Not everyone's success can reach high and tall
Fate is not in our hands
Its upon the sea, if it wants to wash the drawing on the sand

Try to do what you have in control
Don't look back, people are trolls
They bark at success, to stop you from flying
Rather lose from truth than win from lying
It's ok to cry if you lose or go down
But keep a smile, try not to frown
Live every moment and second of life
Together we can pass through this plight

In the end both success and failure,
Both would make you brave here.

6. Hope-A rose!

Hope is like a rose with petals,
So gentle and so free.
Bearing thorns as hard as metal,
Stinging negativity.

Caressing the petals will not make you bleed,
Trying to pluck the rose might.
Hope is always present if you need,
Amidst the darkness, shower light.

The softness of the crimson-red petals
The stinging needle-like thorns.
The sharp edge of leaves, just like nettle,
Hope has no restrictions or bourn.

Hope gives us sight to get through darkness,
A pathway towards light.
Hope is vast and endless,
It's the ability to win our fights.

7. The Colours of Life

The crimson-red of your lips,
As the red, hot winds blow.
Midst the blue sway your hips,
Like gold, your face glows.

Majestic, your black orbs,
That capture in sight.
The beauty this world shows,
The shining white light.

The orange present on the horizon,
Merging with the sea.
Yellow rays emitted by the sun,
Spread your hands, be free.

The mix of shades of pink,
Giving colour to the flowers.
The page of a book, filled with ink,
These shades of life are ours.

8. Hearts of Steel!

We have laptops,
We have robots,
We have beautiful cities.
With no pity.

Unaware of their misery,
We cry over a scraped knee,
We laugh at their pain,
Thinking it's lame.

We make jokes,
While they get soaked,
In the blood they shed,
For our country's welfare.

They leave with big bags,
Saying "I'll try to be back"
Families wait for them to come
Unaware of their martyrdom.

Look at them stand tall!
Knowing anytime death can call.
Keeping in mind, United we stand
Divided we fall.

9. This Motherland is Mine!

In which I confine,
This is my land,
This is my sign,
With respect I fold my hands.

You can smile with no worries,
In past, freedom we sought.
Now we can be in peace,
Because the soldiers they fought.

Why? People thought.
Patriotism arose,
Will power is what,
Over fear they chose.

This is my land,
This is my sign,
In this I confine,
This motherland is mine.

10. Etiquettes

Etiquettes might sound boring,
In our bed, we'd rather be snoring.
But can you live without these rules,
Do you want to be seen like a fool?

School is where you collect your knowledge,
Then you pass on to a fine college.
But still some rules you must maintain,
All these etiquettes will make you stay.

Keep your classroom clean and nice,
So that your classroom is free of mice.
It's cool to be nice and clean,
And give out an aura that is serene.

Raise your hands before answering a question,
Screaming out wouldn't be perfection.
Let the teacher complete her lesson,
So, knowledge is spread around the section.

These are some rules you must follow,
Then you won't have guilt to swallow,
These aren't just rules for school,
These etiquettes will make you cool.

11. True or False?

True or False?
Want to know the truth
Eating a fruit or two
Forgetting you
Is what a false friend would do
But dividing the fruit into two
And eating with you
Is what a true friend would do.

When you are in darkness
They won't lead you to happiness
Push you more towards sadness
Is this what a true friend would do?
When they discourage you
Only he would encourage you
Is this what a false friend would do?
Who is true? Who is false?
A decision you have to do!
Making False preachments
Giving you bad treatment

Are you sure it's true?
On the contrary,
He having a golden heart,
Treating you like his own,
Can't be false of course?

Now what should you do?
It's a decision up to you!

12. The seed-giving father!

During all our highs and lows,
There is always one resort.
The footsteps that have always led you,
And provided you support

Amongst the planets, Earth he is,
Where you could live in peace.
Amongst the stars, sun he is,
Warmth you get and bliss.

Father, you have the greatest heart,
Sacrifices that you do,
For the little girl who once did crawl,
Now wants to be like you.

What else can I convey, for words are small,
To describe you, my dad.
Because of you, I stand so tall,
I hope these words, they make you glad.

13. The arms of a mother!

If you ever feel distressed,
Or your whole mind feels cluttered,
Have you ever tried to find comfort,
In the arms of your mother?

When you are busy outside,
And your life seems filled with colour,
Have you ever thought of the hands that fed you?
The arms of your mother?

All the pain she took,
Is beyond our wonder
Can we appreciate the hardwork of,
The arms of our mother.

Thank you so much to all mothers.
For bearing hunger,
For letting us sleep soundly,
In the arms of our mother.

14. Raksha Bandhan

A festival of bonds, is Raksha Bandhan,
So wake up everyone, wear something nice.
A brother will never abandon,
Just get a Rakhi of his size.

Fights with siblings happen all the time,
But now forget everything replace hatred with love.
Relations are sweet and sour, just like lime,
Try being compatible like a pigeon and a dove.

Siblings are like water and sand,
They don't get mixed.
But in hard times they hold their hand,
Their love for each other is fixed.

White and black, light and dark,
Both of them form a unique contrast.
Love and hate relations is what,
Makes us siblings love at no cost.

15. A token of respect!

"Happy Teacher's Day"
Is what we all should say.
Show respect for throwing light in your life,
Help us go through, and win our fights.

Teachers grant us the right insights,
So that we could soar high like a kite.
Rather than drowning in darkness as black as night,
And in our life, show all our might.

Teacher is another form of god,
Respect them. They deserve to be adored.
No money would amount to the knowledge they give.
We use this knowledge, an important necessity to live.

As a little token of respect and admiration,
Please accept these words I wrote.
A teacher always focusses on precision,
Hence, I raise a toast.

16. Independence Day!

On this honourable day,
Let's show the flag love and care.
And the lives of the soldiers laid,
For the country's welfare.

This country provided shelter for ages,
It's time for us to repay.
This country is known as the land of sages,
'Jai Hind' wouldn't hurt to say.

Orange represents bravery,
White represents peace.
Green represents greenery,
Blue chakra represents an opportunity to seize.

With this in mind, let's look up high,
Our flag, look, it stands up so tall.
Look at how its colours fly,
Come on! Give everyone a call.

17. Reading Day!

The beauty that these words behold,
The magic they contain.
The tales of victors left untold,
The widows who weep in pain.

Gliding through the pages,
Which are smeared with letters of gold.
Some fights with mighty maces,
The stories from ages old.

As our breath hastens,
A new adventure, it unfolds.
The war of mighty nations,
The words that warm the soul.

The depth that these words foster,
The suspense that it creates.
Whether it be terrifying monsters,
Or a lover left dismayed.

The powerful aura they possess,
Timeless, Boundless, Limitless are they.
On this note, to the crowd I address,
A very Happy Reading Day.

18. The Observer

How is life? Hope it's good I pray.
A standard dialogue,we all say.
The person will say yes of course.
But there is a someone, seeing his pain and remorse.

What have we achieved with fake smiles and love?
Will this little act make you somewhat above,
All is seen by this entity
Who observes it all and laughs in pity.

Fights with friends , Fights with enemies,
Disturbing one's inner peace,
We fail to realise better things in life,
And fall into a pit of lies.

We try to find happiness outside,
This is all just a play of mind,
What we were looking for was always in,
The Observer was always within

Indeed we can't control our thoughts,
Observe it, don't act on this a lot.
BE! don't become someone to prove.
The Observer is the real you.

The Observer is unaffected from,
The things we hear on telecom.
The mind is not you, remember this
Who realises this fact, attains eternal bliss.

19. Jai Guru!

One may have the best physique,
And looks which cannot be compared.
One's riches may be at the peak,
One may be prosperity's heir.

One may have the best consort,
One may have no foes.
One may be loved by all,
One may have the best of clothes.

But what use is all this material attraction,
This will end one day too.
Instead shift your focus,
To the lotus feet of the Guru.

They teach us how to live,
They teach us how to behave.
They teach us to commit,
To promises we once made.

This material world will end,
But these teachings they last forever,
Gurus are godsent,
To them we must surrender.

I thank my gurus,
For they sought my welfare.
I thank my gurus,
For their unwavering care.

20. The Voice of the Dead!

There he was, once full of life
Now on the ground he laid.
Cotton swabs, cloth satin white.
All happiness did fade.

He looks here and there, everywhere,
Confused, and in dismay.
The cries, the screams, the misery
He thought what a silly play!

He sees his wife, clad in white
A tear drops right from her eye
He calls out to her, "My dear, my dear!"
"Why is it that you cry"

Silence was all he heard,
He shouted and he screamed,
Was this a joke, a play of mind
Or maybe just a dream.

He looks down to see, a man who's freed,
From the clutches of material life,
"But why does he look like me"
Realization struck him like a knife.

"That can't be me....why do you cry!"
A small hope, that it's a lie.
How can he say, how can he prove
"I'm breathing...I'm alive!!"

Noone knows, when death arrives,
There's no time to even flinch.
Once, that man was full of life,
Now couldn't move an inch.

21. Inner Journey

When I was a child,
Everything seemed happy.
Whether I lost a race.
Or won a trophy.

I was imperfect,
In every single way.
Whether it be looks,
Or the way that I play.

Now I have everything I wanted,
Everything I dreamt,
Has fallen into place.
Yet I lament.

I looked for the reason,
I tried to understand why.
Why I was ungrateful,
When there's no reason to cry.

I peeked into those eyes,
The eyes which knew no sin,
I spent my life searching outside,
For what was always within.

I do have family,
I do have friends.
Yet I feel alone,
It doesn't make any sense.

Suddenly everything crashed,
My life was in shambles.
I focused on the inner self,
He guided me through all my 'rambles'.

Now I feel nothing,
Whether I win or lose
Maintaining the serenity,
The Inner journey I choose!

22. INDIA-2050

Have you ever wondered,
What the future would look like?
Flying cars, flying skates,
Or maybe a flying bike.

Robots as your servants,
For everything you do.
Digitalized and easy living,
There's nothing you have to do.

The finest quality of food,
The finest shoes to step,
Will everything glimmer and shine?
Or be something we don't expect?

Lazy, dependant public,
Rising crime rate,
Technology is all we know,
Should this be our fate?

No more fresh air, no more love,
No more human connect.
All we have known our entire lives,
Is a device with no 'defect'.

The rich history of India,
How soldiers fought with crooks,
Worthy of immense respect!
Now lie in a dusted book.

Men lying on the streets,
Women crying in pain.
Technology taking over jobs,
Humanity is slain.

Is this all worth it?
Is this wanted by you?
Do you want to stay in this future,
Or pave a way for something new?

23. Bharat!

The land of cultural heritage
The land where knowledge dawn's
The land of liberated sages
The land where I was born

The sacred land of India
Is as old as old can be
The manuscripts with eternal knowledge
To be free from all misery

But indeed tragedy struck
As crooks did try to loot
The richness that did exist
Was claimed by men in suits.

After ages of being ruled,
After years of tyranny,
Patriotism arose
A will to become free

And when our flag rose high
Higher than the skies
Several voices cried
Regaining the lost pride!

This day is indeed historic
A day when we regained,
Freedom, Liberty and Love
Prosperity showered like rain!

24. Red or Blue?

Little Johnny went to sleep,
He dreamt that he could fly,
The next day he jumped out of the
window,
Johnny almost died.

Susan dreamt that she could jump
Higher than the sky,
She jumped and jumped for so much
time,
Now she's got a sore thigh.

Amber dreamt that Gordon ate her pizza,
So she took a stick to beat.
Gordon cried out with a broken tooth, Salads were all he
could eat.

To dream is not wrong,

It's an expression of our mind.
But thinking all of it could be true,
Is impractical and a waste of time.

That doesn't mean you leave behind,
Your ambitions and your dreams.
But be mentally prepared for highs and lows,
Success isn't as easy as it seems.

Have you ever thought about?
How many people share the same passion?
Do you have what it takes to be,
One in a million or billion?

This is not to discourage you,
Or completely abandon your desire.
Lead life steadily with simplicity.
Execute it and admire.

You have two options at this point,
A red or a blue pill,
The blue one you choose to avoid the risk,
The red one to be fulfilled.

25. The Spirit of Devotion

Like the sand on the seashore
Is washed away by the ocean
The land of misery
Is transcended by the spirit of devotion

Oh lord! Grant everyone sight
To free us from the cycle or life
Should I be engulfed in the darkness of
the night
Or be blinded by the sun rays so bright

The Art of Living,
Is not merely a course.
It's to be elevated,
And giving in to the almighty's force.

Hence I plead
Be free from all notions
Arise within
The Spirit of Devotion!

26. The Best friend of Death!

The little boy stared blankly,
With his lifeless eyes,
A tall, shadowy figure appeared
Saying Its time for your demise".

Innocently, the little boy asked,
"What is this demise you speak of?"
"And why do you wear a cloak as dark"
"As my room when the lights are off?"

The man just laughed a little and said
"Fate indeed was unfair,
A little boy like you should relish life
And not be in the clutches of despair."

The little boy held his hand,
And asked "What is death?"
"That's my name" the man replied
"I take people low on health"

The little boy said that
"The whole world is scared of you,
They create new technologies
To get away from you.

The man says in response,
"Noone can escape this reality
Whether it be a baby, maiden or old
aged men,
The whole of humanity."

The little boy chuckled a bit
And said, "You are similar to me..
I always have to keep going
Regardless of he or she"

"And people call me their enemy
Because I wait for none,
And people always race me till
They reach end of the run"

That's when the man realized.
He was no ordinary lad,
Could he be a demigod?
Or a human who is mad?

"I am the vital force of nature,
The most powerful of them all,
I was never born nor do I have an end,
Nor can I fly nor fall"

That's when the man realised that,
It was his best friend indeed
Both of them, feared by all,
But they never paid heed.

"As innocent as a little boy,
Dutiful, inevitable, I am,
The most feared and most powerful
Time I am!"

27. I wish!

I wish that I was in a world,
Where without worries I could twirl,
Rejoice in peace and be free,
Devoid of orthodox caste or creed.

I wish that the world was less complex,
Without any unnecessary stress,
A world where I could be anything
Where I could dance and
could sing.

I wish no one knew what tears are,
There is only love, there would be no
scars.
Forever young, Forever alive,
All of us would together thrive.

These wishes remain unfulfilled
But with satisfaction, my heart is
filled.

I tried finding happiness in every little
thing I sought,
Inner peace, I finally got.

28. SPECIAL SECTION 1- POEMS ON WEDNESDAY ADDAMS

Wednesday is an American coming-of-age supernatural mystery television series based on the character Wednesday Addams by Charles Addams. But these poems are specifically based on Wednesday series from Netflix. These poems revolve around two love interests of Wednesday, Xavier and Tyler. Tyler was a boy who worked at a cafe and Xavier

studied at Nevermore. Nevermore was a school for different type of monsters. A series of murders took place whose culprit was the monster, Hyde. In the end, Tyler turned out to be Hyde. But it was not his fault. His mother also was possessed by Hyde. He never realised that but Wednesday's dorm mother, Marilyn Thornhill, wanted to use him for this,

She began to plot her revenge to kill all outcasts and destroy Nevermore Academy, doing what her brother and

father failed to do. Her real name was Laurel Gates.

28. Xavier's POV

Your black, doe eyes
Contrast to your pale skin
People, you despise
Attracted towards sin

Your tender body
Hiding toughness within
All your opponents quite sorry
For messing with your kin

Your soft, red lips
Smeared with blood
Of the people you killed
Their screams left unheard

To you I give signs
You, who drinks blood instead of wine
So Ms. Wednesday Addams
I, Xavier, Ask you to be mine

29. Wednesday and Tyler- Two broken Hearts!

Blonde, curly locks of hair,
Adorning his face,
His skin tone quite fair,
He makes Wednesday's heart increase its pace.

His large, hazel doe eyes,
Searching far someone true,
Unknowingly being fed white lies,
People like him, quit few.

Just a regular waiter was he,
At a small bistro shop.
Fate made them meet,
Through a simple cop.

Laurel had kidnapped him,
Knowing he was the son of Hyde.
Made him her little slave,
Bringing about a destructive tide.

Poor Wednesday, unaware of this
Fell in love with this guy,
But soon did the secret unleash,
A web of deception, a big lie!

She did fight him with all her might,
He did face several blows,
Every hit did stab her heart,
Tears like river flowed.

She did succeed saving Nevermore,
A huge sacrifice, her love.
But this was what she knew was right,
Her feelings she did shove.

This is how two hearts broke,
For the world to be saved.
Wednesday and Tyler both went about,
Their different lives and ways.

30. SPECIAL SECTION 2- THE VISION OF A JOURNALIST

"The Vision of a Journalist" discusses different events that took place specifically in India. Here, "Journalism" indicates unaltered truth, which offers a perspective on each event. This series is dedicated to these horrifying events.

Imagine a journalist with a little brown book and a pen present at each of these events. This journalist stands and stares but has no right to alter history. All that journalist can do is write about these events poetically and present it to the audience. I hope you enjoy reading it!

30. The Bhopal Gas Tragedy!

When the sky had turned all black,
I woke up just to see.
The people, crowd were lying down,
The station master on his knees,

All it took was just one breath,
And I felt a little faint,
Was it dust? Or the smell of smoke?
Or the pungent smell of paint

Realization struck,
When I did look the other side,
The monster had been now unleashed,
A Leak from Union Carbide.

I quickly tore a piece of cloth.
And bound it 'round my face.
People screamed, some yelped in pain,
And the crowd had rushed to race.

We all gathered in the waiting room.
As the stationmaster limped,
Along with two more young workers,
Their skin had turned all pink

Even in their last.
Did they try to save some lives,
As they tried to communicate.
To people unaware of this demise.

My eyes had now turned bloodshot red.
As they peeked through the glass to see,
Millions of them lying dead,
As if the corpses formed a sea.

As I saw foam dripping down.
From the victims' mouths,
The wind which flowed had now carried,
The gas from north and south.

Stationmaster had assembled the train,
And helped everybody in.
But he himself went in the search,
For some more of our kin.

I quickly took out my camera,

To capture this tragedy,
The factory was like a rusted lock,
Which could open without a key.

No safety precaution, nor masks, nor gloves,
Could now save the city,
All we could do was watch and stare,
The deaths of men in pity.

But then did lord send some help,
From the neighbouring stations,
And now the horrid night had passed.
Free from this monstrous incarnation.

And I did type an article,
For this was not to be ignored,
A matter of 15000 lives,
And several families tore.

As desired, the factory shut down,
People gained their sanity,
And now this unforgettable trauma,
Is labelled as the Bhopal Gas Tragedy.

-Inspired by 'The Railway Men' .
Based on True Events.

31. Its always her....

Just another day, another night,
She's working in the dark.
And then did he destroy her life
He left a brutal mark.

Her father had come to see,
The daughter whom he cherished
To his horror, the door revealed
The girl was dead, completely perished

She was raped, she was butchered
She did try to scream.
But nothing could stop this monster,
From murdering all her dreams.

A doctor always gives us hope,
A hope that helps us strive.
Yet this man took away,
That very soul which gives us life

Fie on humanity!! Fie on us!!
To this level we have descent.
Where everyone blames the girl who died
And the man does not repent.

In the end, the girl now watches
This corrupt society
She went through hell, she went through pain
While he roams on the streets.

32. The Jalianwala Bagh Tragedy

33. 26/11- Mumbai Reborn!

Clock struck 6 as I got off to my desired station,
The City where one yearns to go, The pride of our nation.
Suddenly we hear gunshots which never seemed to stop.
Then I see a heap of bodies, some with body parts all chopped.

The stations filled with panic and people screaming sickly.
I take my camera and capture this horrifying show quickly.
I find a place to hide and see the ones who caused this act
A bunch of teens with guns nurtured with the wrong facts.

They left no trace of life and went to their next location.
Leopold cafe was next as they mutilated the station.
I came out of hiding and what I saw left me mortified.
Kids, Ladies, Men some injured, dead, left me horrified.

I saw on the TV that they had butchered their next site.
How vile were they! To shamelessly stare at this
petrifying sight.
I find out that they were a Pakistani Terrorist Group,
When young, they're brainwashed and pulled into this
vicious coup.

They went to Oberoi, Trident and The Taj Palace Hotel,
They inhumanly destroyed the places where we dwelled.
The Cama hospital and St.Xavier's College.
What could we do by blaming them! Fie on their
knowledge!

Yet it took three days for us to manage this circumstance.
It was our fault to even give them such a chance.
This was a matter of more than hundreds who were
dead.
While their killers, for three whole days, freely fled.

Through bullets and corpses, we were reborn.
Our spirit was high, united and sworn.
For even amidst the horror and pain,
Mumbai's indomitable spirit shall always reign.

33. SPECIAL SECTION 3- Hindu Mythology

This section specifically includes poems related to Indian Mythology.
Indian mythology is an intricate tapestry of stories, beliefs, and cultural wisdom that has been woven over millennia. It is deeply rooted in philosophy, spirituality, and morality, offering profound insights into human nature, the cosmos, and the divine.
Indian mythology is a vast and fascinating world filled with incredible stories, powerful gods and goddesses, and deep philosophical ideas. Here's a little peek into what makes it so special:

Key Aspects:

- **Ancient Roots:**Indian mythology is deeply rooted in ancient texts like the Vedas, the epics Ramayana and Mahabharata, and the Puranas. These texts are thousands of years old!
- **A World of Deities:**It features a rich pantheon of gods and goddesses, each with unique powers and

personalities. Some of the most well-known include:

- Brahma (the creator)
- Vishnu (the preserver)
- Shiva (the destroyer)
- Ganesha (the remover of obstacles)
- Lakshmi (the goddess of prosperity)

- Saraswati (the goddess of knowledge)
- **Epic Tales:**The Ramayana and Mahabharata are two of the world's greatest epic poems. They tell stories of heroes, battles, and the struggle between good and evil. These stories teach important lessons about duty, courage, and righteousness.
- **Symbolism and Meaning:**Indian mythology is full of symbolism. The stories often have deeper meanings that explore philosophical and spiritual concepts.
- **Diversity:**Because India is such a large and diverse country, there are many regional variations of these myths and legends. This adds to the richness and complexity of Indian mythology.

Why it's important:

- These stories have played a huge role in shaping Indian culture and traditions.

- They continue to inspire people with their timeless messages and powerful imagery.
- It is a very large part of the culture of a very large portion of the worlds population.

34. Krishna- Divinity Personified!

A peacock feather adorning his hair,
Dark-skinned yet always fair!
His flute fixated on his lips.
The gopis enchanted, lost in eternal bliss!

He held no grudges, he held no hate
He accepted what was accorded by fate!
For his birth was for a special cause
As righteousness came to a sudden pause!

The ones who died were liberated indeed
From the clutches of life they were freed!
As they merged into "singularity"
A feeling of tranquility!

Oh Krishna! You reside in our hearts!
You guide us, bring us to the start.
Yet we're unable to detach,
Ourselves from this lustful latch!

A smile that never leaves his face,
His name that gives us solace!
The embodiment of divinity!
Oh Krishna! I give in to your serenity!

||JAI SHREE KRISHNA||

35. The Tale of Rama

In the kingdom of Ayodhya,
Thus was born,
A boy named Rama,
With a Crown to be adorned !

Alas, fate did betray,
The king's hopes all killed.
To everyone's utter dismay,
The queen with hatred got filled

Exiled for 14 years,
With his beautiful wife,
Sita, who shed no tears,
For the hardships in life.

A knock on the door,
Came a rakshas in disguise,
With the face of a brahmin,
Begging for rice

Innocent was Sita,
Who fell for his trap,
Mighty Ravana was he,
The fish was in his catch.

She screamed and she shrieked,
"You wretched, You fool"
"You'll never be successfull"
"In what you seek"...

He laughed at her comments,
And threw her in a forest,
As she wondered and cried,
How her beloved she met.

Rama was engulfed,
In the arms of grief,
As tears rolled down,
Like dew drops on leaf

He built an army of monkeys,
And trained them to fight,
They crossed the mighty sagar,
Entered Lanka, the land of light.

The war raged on,
For many days to come,

Atlast the arrow hit,
And killed the environment so glum.

Everyone rejoiced,
As Ravana was slaid,
Except his beautiful wife.
Who watched from the shade.

Atlast they met,
After days of seperation,
Imagining their future to come,
And the upcoming generations.

This tale of love,
Illuminates the world,
And shines brighter than the sun,
The name is Ramayan..

36. Karna- The Unfortunate Warrior!

The poem I am about to share is about a character that has left an ever-lasting impression on my heart! Not only me but millions of people due to his noble character! His misfortune and his pain often have the power to move people. Even though he was on the wrong side due to his oath, he gained immense respect from Lord Krishna himself. He spared the lives of his brothers despite his oath, he sacrificed his life for his friendship!

This is how Lord Krishna described him:
"As righteous as Yudhishthir, As strong as Bhima, Archery like that of Arjuna, Handsomeness of Nakul and Premonition like that of Sahadev!"

This is none other than the eldest of Pandavas, the forlorn son of Kunti:
KARNA

The story of a warrior,

The story of his pain,
The story of his faults,
In this story, he is slain.

Descending on earth,
He shone as bright as the sun.
With divine earings and armour,
The result of her fun.

At birth he was abandoned,
In the river he was thrown.
Found by a charioteer,
As 'Radheya' was he known.

As curly locks of hair,
Adorned his face.
The aura of the Sun,
Worthy of praise!

Born as a kshatriya,
Living as a suta.
Fate always played against,
This Kuntiputra.

He ascended the arena,
Gracefully aimed the bow.
Performed extraordinary feats,

Amazing his foes.

For his caste he was judged,
His talent was forgotten.
Publicly insulted,
The society was rotten.

But only one man then,
Adorned him with a crown.
His name was Duryodhana,
The elders did frown.

Seeing this act,
Radheya's eyes surely filled.
He took an oath of friendship,
Until he was killed.

When his eyes laid on Kunti,
A strange bond he felt.
Her eyes filled with guilt.
Her heart did melt.

He went to a swayamvar,
With might lifted the bow.
His aim was precise,
Suddenly, a voice screamed "NO".

Draupadi did insult,
This warrior indeed.
Eventhough at first look,
He surely did please.

She mocked him publicly,
His heart yearned for revenge.
A fire arose within.
Which needed to be quenched.

It was not the rejection,
But the insults that were thrown.
What use was his archery?
What use was his gold?

During the game of dice,
Draupadi was then bet.
He called her a harlot
He surely did regret .

Krishna stood for peace,
Radheya tried to explain.
But Duryodhana was blinded,
Rage made him insane.

Radheya knew he was wrong,
But as if bound by karma.

The ropes of this friendship,
Pulled him away from dharma.

Krishna visited Radheya,
Revealed his identity.
Radheya sunk in grief,
How he wished he could flee!

Then Kunti did visit,
Her forlorn son.
His radiance indeed,
Was unmatched like the sun!

She pleaded him thus!
She told him that he would
Be the eldest of Pandavas!
Rule Aryavart because he could!

He would be free from insults,
Draupadi would be his wife.
His five brothers for protection,
Free from all strife!

Yet he didn't betray his friend,
He refused to change his path.
Made a promise to never kill,
Anyone but Parth!

Indra approached Radheya in disguise.
Made use of his generosity.
He cut through his ears, his chest was bare.
Indra was filled with pity.

He offered him the eternal vajra,
Only once at his command.
Would kill the foe precisely but,
Fate robbed it off his hands

Shailya was his charioteer,
Who demotivated him thus.
He ignored it all and fought with tact,
Forgetting all the fuss.

He knew that indeed,
In this war he would die.
Yet he fought for his friend,
Whom he could never deny!

The 17th day of war!
He stood face to face
Was he his foe?
Or a brotherly image?

Vijay vs Gandiva!

Both fought with great might!
All the demigods overlooked,
The majestic, yet feirce sight!

Radheyas chariot got stuck,
So he got down to free
As shailya refused,
To perform this deed.

That's when Govind,
Ordered arjuna to aim!
But how could he kill,
A warrior with no weopons to claim!

He reminded Arjuna.
Of Karna's misdeeds
The arrow left his quiver,
Radheya did bleed!

He smiled as the arrow pierced,
He fell with a thud!
He was happy to die,
At the hands of his blood!

Only one question did,
Linger in his mind,
Will the world know his competence,

Will the world ever be kind?

Vasudev then said!
"We had to kill you when you
Were weaoponless and vulnerable!
Isnt that enough proof "

Radheya then smiled,
Amidst all his griefs
Offered his obesiances
He felt immense relief!

That day the sun set early,
To mourn for his son!
He may have lost the war!
But millions of hearts he won!

This was the story of,
The descendant of the Sun!
You may call him Radheya,
Or Kuntiputra Karn!

37. The Arrows That Struck My Heart! -Arjuna's POV

The day that I have waited for, The day I take his life,
The day I kill the charioteer's son, The day I avenge my wife!
With Hanuman mounting on my flag and Madhav by my side
Yet I feel so uneasy every time my aim is precise!

Surely, he put up a fierce fight, as his arrows crashed with mine,
He smiled; every time my arrows left a bloody sign!
Suddenly his chariot's wheels start digging in the earth.
He got down to lift his chariot, which was his duty by birth!

His bow was in his chariot and both his hands were tied.
Then Keshav ordered me to shoot, for there would be no better time!
Suddenly I'm taken back to all of his misdeeds.
The arrow left my quiver, now from life, the Suta was

freed!

As my arrow pierced his neck, a tear fell right from her
eye
I wondered! Why my mother wept...when the foe had
died!
I asked "Oh Mother! Your son's sole enemy lies here
dead!"
She stopped...as Karna held her hand, smiled and shook
his head

My mother turned towards him and said "Son this is the
time,
"They deserve to know the truth, this fatal mistake of
mine!"
My brothers and I stared at his mangled body which still
had some life,
As our mother clung to his body, had she forgotten about
our wife?

Then her voice shook as she said the following words:
"Karna is not a suta but the eldest Pandava by birth!"
My eyes it filled with tears, My mouth, it felt so dry.
He was not my foe, my elder brother I had defied!

My breathing, it slowed down, My Gandiva, then it fell,
I would have rather died; my life was now a living hell.

He knew the truth and let us live, yet he put me through the pain!
Of what use is my power, my archery? All of it felt vain!

Later that night after my elder's corpse was burnt.
I cursed myself! I could never give the love for which he yearned!
Then I saw my radiant brother descend from the sky!
He said "My dear brother! There is no reason to cry!"

I shouted, "How could you be so selfish to put me through this pain!"
"If only I had known the truth! I would have never slain!"
He smiled and then he stared at me, with his gleaming eyes.
As golden locks of his hair, they swayed from time to time

"Just a little hint, a little word...would've destroyed all the 'heat ' "
Then my Gandiva would lie there, right at your feet"
I wished to say a lot, yet words, my tongue it failed to utter!
I wept and wept, he stared at me as his eyes it fluttered!

He said "My dearest brother! For my adharma, I had to

pay the fine!"
"I knew that you would surrender if I ever called you mine!"
"Then who would give justice to Panchali's open hair?"
"And how could I ascend the throne when Yudhistir's the rightful heir!"

"If you would've joined our side, we would've showered you with love!
With me and Bheem as your protectors! We five would place you above!"
He shook his head and said, "Oh the greatest archer of all time!"
"My hands were tied; my lips were sealed with this friendship oath of mine!"

"But now I am freed from the bondage of my life!"
"I wished for death by your hands, not death at someone's knife!'
"Now embrace me dear! This was a wish that I surely failed to fulfill!"
"I would have blessed you then if it was not against my will!"

I ran and I embraced him; I kept tugging at his arms!
My eldest brother stood right there with no intent to harm!

The next moment, I saw his radiance, it slowly vanished.
And that is how my eldest brother, from my life, was
banished!

38. The Spark of War- Disrobing of a women's pride!

I held my husband's hands as I did climb the stairs,
As my hair it flew in accordance with the air!
Duryodhana along with his brothers, respect and love they lent!
But something felt wrong in the love they did present!

After some entertainment, they said we'll keep a game of dice,
Were they showing love? Or entrapping us in a web of lies!
They said "All women must be escorted in a room!"
I wish I had known this was the way to my doom!

In the start, it felt so harmless, they were betting on some gold!
But every single time, my husband, he had to fold.
I kept complete faith, I knew that he would draw the

line!
I prayed to lord hoping everything would be fine!

The news I heard next then shook me deep inside!
He had lost the kingdom and my other husbands rights!
And the next thing I knew he had now lost his own life!
And now he was forced to stake me, Panchali, his wife!

I waited for a while and then I heard banging on the door.
The banging was followed by heavy thumping on the floor.
The court had now been tainted with the marks of an evil sin
I turned around to see Dushasan, waiting with a grin.

He said "You were lost in this game and now you belong to us!"
"You have been ordered to follow me without any fuss!"
I screamed "With what right was I staked and bet in this game!"
"What sort of treachery is done tainting 'dharma's' name!"

Saying this I stormed out as rage they filled my eyes..
But then I felt a sudden pull right from behind.
My hair was being pulled as I was dragged right in

between!
And the court it remained silent, as silent as it could be.

My hair it lied open, a bruise near my lips...
My head with a wound, a piece of cloth covering my hips.
I shouted "O King dhritrashtra! The public shall blame you for in your reign,"
"The court lost all its shame to witness this ugly scene!"

"Oh Pitamah! Aren't I Hastinapur's pride!"
"Yet you lie helpess and watch me be defied!"
"Oh Guru Dron! You deem me to be your daughter!"
"And yet you seem so silent as my honour gets slaughtered!"

I wait for a response, I had pleaded all to help
Except the charioteer's son, for there was no use, i felt!
He stood up and said "A lady can have husbands, only four!"
"What honour! A girl with five husbands is a whore!"

And the entire court it burst into laughter except the three,
Bhisma, Drona Karna...just sat helplessly to see.
And then Duryodhana he shouted "Sit on my thigh!"
"I would protect you better than your husbands five!"

I looked at him in fiery and I saw his lust fade!
Duryodhana blinded by rage said "Strip this arrogant maid!"
I joined my hands and chanted "Govinda! Help your friend!"
"And surely soon this evil men will have to make amends"

As Dushasana tried, my clothes it never left my side...
It was Madhav's miracle indeed! Dushasan's pride it slowly died...
I, then left the kingdom, my husbands heads they hung down in shame.
Five warrior husbands! Yet all their valour was in vain!

And this act set in stone a war noone could ever forget...
'Mahabharat' is how adharma, with the end it surely met!